My Emotions Through Emojis

FEELING SAD

BY
THEIA LAKE

Enslow PUBLISHING

Please visit our website, www.enslow.com.
For a free color catalog of all our high-quality books, call toll free 1-800-398-2504 or fax 1-877-980-4454.

Cataloging-in-Publication Data
Names: Lake, Theia.
Title: Feeling sad / Theia Lake.
Description: New York : Enslow Publishing, 2024. | Series: My emotions through emojis | Includes index.
Identifiers: ISBN 9781978533455 (pbk.) | ISBN 9781978533462 (library bound) | ISBN 9781978533479 (ebook)
Subjects: LCSH: Sadness in children–Juvenile literature. | Sadness–Juvenile literature. | Emotions in children–Juvenile literature.
Classification: LCC BF723.S15 L35 2023 | DDC 155.4'124–dc23

Published in 2024 by
Enslow Publishing
2544 Clinton Street
Buffalo, NY 14224

Designer: Tanya Dellaccio Keeney
Editor: Theresa Emminizer

Photo credits: Cover (phone) Victor Z/Shutterstock.com; cover, series art (clouds) Theus/Shutterstock.com; cover, series art (emojis) stas11/Shutterstock.com; p. 5 Luis Molinero/Shutterstock.com; p. 7 Volodymyr TVERDOKHLIB/Shutterstock.com; pp. 9, 11 Ground Picture/Shutterstock.com; p. 13 EZ-Stock Studio/Shutterstock.com; pp. 15, 17 fizkes/Shutterstock.com; p. 19 balanser/Shutterstock.com; p. 21 Prostock-studio/Shutterstock.com.

Printed in the United States of America

CPSIA compliance information: Batch #CS24ENS: For further information contact Enslow Publishing, at 1-800-398-2504.

CONTENTS

Boldface words appear in Words to Know.

A HARD FEELING

We all have lots of different feelings inside us. Sometimes we're happy. Sometimes we're mad. Sometimes we're sad. Feeling sad can be hard. But it's important to know you won't always feel that way. Remember, feelings come and feelings go.

IN YOUR BODY

How does sadness feel? When you're sad, your body might feel heavy. You might feel tired. Maybe your throat feels tight and your eyes fill with tears. Let your tears fall! Crying can help you feel better.

IT'S OKAY TO CRY

Cole's dog is lost 😔. She's been gone for two days, and Cole **worries** he'll never see her again. Cole tries not to cry 😖. He's scared that crying means he's **weak** or babyish. He hides his face.

Cole's friend asks him if he's okay. She tells him to go ahead and cry if he feels like it! Cole cries 😭. He tells his friend about his worries. After, he feels much better. It's like a little bit of the sadness has left him ☹️.

SHARE YOUR FEELINGS

When we're sad, it can really help to tell someone. It doesn't matter if they can't fix what's going on. Just sharing what you're feeling can help make it better. You'll feel less alone. You'll understand your own feelings better.

DON'T HIDE IT

Bella's been feeling very sad lately 😢. Her parents are getting **divorced**. Bella misses living with her dad. She feels like her family is broken 😩. But Bella is scared to share her feelings with her mom and dad. She hides the sadness inside.

YOU'RE NOT ALONE

It can be hard to tell people how we feel. Even people we love! We might worry they'll be mad. If you can't talk to your parents, find another adult you trust. Maybe a teacher or another family member. You're not alone.

EXPRESS YOURSELF

Jasper's grandma **passed away** last spring. Sometimes he feels very sad about it ☹️. When he gets sad, it helps Jasper to write about his feelings 😔. It's like the sadness leaves his body and goes onto the pages of his **journal**.

FEEL YOUR FEELINGS

Nobody likes feeling sad. But you don't have to hide your feelings or wish them away. You can let yourself feel sad knowing that you aren't alone and that it will pass. Feeling sad is part of life, and that's okay!

WORDS TO KNOW

divorce: Ending a marriage or splitting up.

journal: A notebook in which people write thoughts or feelings.

pass away: To die.

weak: Not strong.

worry: To think about problems or things you are afraid of.

FOR MORE INFORMATION

BOOKS

Moore-Mallinos, Jennifer. *Mad, Frustrated, and Sad.* New York, NY: Windmill Books, 2019.

Wood, John. *Sam the Sloth Feels Sad.* New York, NY: Windmill Books, 2020.

WEBSITES

British Council
learnenglishkids.britishcouncil.org/songs/feelings-are-feelings
Listen to songs and play games about feelings.

Kids Health
kidshealth.org/en/kids/talk-feelings.html
Learn how to name and talk about your feelings.

Publisher's note to educators and parents: Our editors have carefully reviewed these websites to ensure that they are suitable for students. Many websites change frequently, however, and we cannot guarantee that a site's future contents will continue to meet our high standards of quality and educational value. Be advised that students should be closely supervised whenever they access the internet.

INDEX